Contents

D1632637

Acknowledgements

Photographs by Bob Willingham, to whom goes the author's especial gratitude for his distinctive contribution. Thanks also to Paul Tiley and Neil Beckett of Bath Judo Club for their tireless and enthusiastic modelling, and to Kim Willingham and to Diki Gleeson.

Note   Throughout the book participants are referred to individually as 'he'. This should, of course, be taken to mean 'he or she' where appropriate.

Foreword

In 1975 I wrote in the foreword of Geof Gleeson's book *All About Judo* that it might contain his final comments on his revolutionary approach to the teaching of judo. Fortunately, he lived long enough to construct this remarkable enhancement of his earlier books – enhanced by the brilliant photographs of Bob Willingham. The pictures are a vivid expression of Geof's teaching: that judo need not begin with the static repetitions. They illustrate the way in which inspired teaching can introduce the dynamics of modern competitive judo as the earliest basis for future skill – a precept which confirms why Geof was rightly called 'The foremost judo thinker in the world'. Read this book and compare the illustrations with the very latest photographs of world champions in action.

Let movement be your inspiration.

Jerry Hicks MBE
7th Dan

Introduction

Judo was 'invented' in 1882 in Japan, by a man named Jigoro Kano. It was initially intended to be a means by which young men could be taught social morality through combat training. Gradually it changed in nature and purpose to become a sport. The rate of change was accelerated after World War II, until judo became a world and Olympic sport. Men's judo was introduced at the 1964 Tokyo Olympics, and eventually women's judo was introduced at the Games in Barcelona in 1992.

Judo can be a recreational pastime, a method of self-defence or a competitive sport. Judo skills, like other skills, are learnt differently by different people. In the short term, some learn quickly and others slowly, but in the longer term all can reach whatever level of performance the individual requires. It needs determination.

To begin, ensure that you have access to the correct equipment. You will need a judo suit, as illustrated in all the photographs and available in most sports shops. At this stage it will help too if you can find a friend, or friends, to keep you company and to help you learn.

You will also need a mat and a good coach. The best way to find both of these is by joining a judo club. If you do not know one, contact one of the national judo organisations (the oldest is the British Judo Association) or get in touch with UK Sport (national or regional).

At your club, ensure that the mat you will be using is large, flat and soft (but not spongy). The coach should be interested in you and in your needs; he should be knowledgeable, but have a mind that is open to new ideas – a good coach is one who is continually learning his profession.

Getting started

Starting judo is all about learning. Learning to be effective needs to be planned. So here I offer you a plan, based on many years of judo teaching in many parts of the world. It is very flexible, and can be modified easily to suit individual needs. After a few weeks you may well want to alter it slightly; by all means do so, preferably with the help of an understanding coach.

- Learn how to move in a 'judo' style.
- Observe carefully what happens as you are learning.
- Draw conclusions and memorise them.
- Learn some standard techniques for certain standard situations.
- Learn how to link movement and technique.
- Develop tactical skills.

There are two main divisions of action in judo training: one is concerned with throwing; the other with grappling on the ground. Quite quickly, however, they must be merged and it should be difficult to see the join.

It does not really matter which you start with. In general, young people prefer throwing and older people prefer to grapple. Each has its own advantages and disadvantages. I shall begin as tradition dictates – with throwing.

Learning to move: throwing

A judo skill consists of two elements: *movement* (of the two players) and *technique* (application of the right amount of force, through the body, to the partner so that he falls down or is incapacitated in a hold). It is essential that both these be understood equally, but movement is possibly the most important – by a whisker! – simply because it is the more difficult of the two both to explain and to comprehend.

To start, hold your partner as shown in fig. 1 (*see* page 6). Relax. Now move around the mat, covering the whole area, as if you are ballroom dancing. Experiment by first following the movements of your partner and then purposefully doing something different – so that the movement patterns become jerky and broken instead of smooth and continuous.

Next, experiment with changes in speed. Move quickly and then slowly. Move at the same speed as your partner, then at a different speed. Watch how these changes affect the movement patterns, and try to memorise them. This will prove important when you begin to throw (fig. 1).

Incorporate the element of *strength*, or (the preferable term) *power*. Pull and push each other, first with both hands simultaneously and then with each hand separately. What happens to your partner? Notice how you 'instinctively' pull or push when your partner is doing nothing. (It is important to be aware of this.) Do you prefer to pull when your partner is moving forwards or backwards? Can you make your partner change direction? If so, remember how: it will prove important when devising tactics later in the learning process.

Try making yourself 'heavy' (*see* fig. 2, page 6). In this position you need to pull and push with more power. Try it; feel it, remember it. Again, use both hands together, then separately; strongly, then lightly. Is it easy to move when crouching? Or is it better to move slowly?

Finally, combine all these experiences: fast, slow; heavy, light; crouching, upright. They will all affect the type of throw you use, and its efficacy, so remember what happens and what it feels like.

Learning to move: grappling

These unique pictures are to generate a mood, a realisation of the pace and beauty of judo movement. They are not to show technique but rather to create images of action in your mind: red is for fast; white for medium; and blue for slow. The ability of the player to move at different speeds, to understand the effect of speed on technique, is very important. When you move, feel the movement, enjoy the beauty of moving at various speeds, feel how the different movements take you into the different techniques, for both attack and defence. Movement creates technique. As you learn the many techniques, think of the speed at which they will need to be carried out. If you keep linking movement and technique in this way you will quickly develop skill.

Fig. 6   Blue is for slow; notice how much closer to the ground the foot-roll throw keeps both competitors. Think what kind of advantages that gives both.

Fig. 1   'Tossing their heads in sprightly dance' (Wordsworth). The speed gives you no time to think.

Fig. 2   'And we must take the current when it serves' (Shakespeare). The slower action gives you time to think!

Fig. 3   'Fingers and fingernails seek sound' (Hiroshi Iwata). Grappling at speed – make your own patterns.

Fig. 4   The 'red' speed blurs what you see, but helps you do a foot trip.

Fig. 5   The normal 'white' speed may still not let you see clearly, but, having done the legs-astride throw, it shows you how to start grappling.

▲ *Fig. 1*   ▼ *Fig. 2*

▲ *Fig. 3*

▲ *Fig. 5*

▼ *Fig. 4*

▼ *Fig. 6*

Start off as illustrated in fig. 3 (*see page 7*). Without letting go of your partner's jacket, roll around. Roll over one another, first quickly and then slowly. Feel how the distance between your bodies changes depending on the speed at which you move. Notice that the power to turn you over comes from the feet and legs: remember all the ways in which you use them.

Try letting go with one hand and using it to help turn you both over. Maintain a tight grip with the other. Keep changing speed and direction.

Next, change hands (keep a tight grip on your partner's jacket with one hand, so that he cannot 'run away') and use the free hand to move him.

Add power. At this point stop just 'moving around' and try to give a focus to the movement. At no time must either man allow the flat of his back to stay on the mat. Once either player feels his back on the mat he must twist, roll, turn and push (with the feet and the hands) to get off his back and on to his side or his front.

Finish by going back to speed work. Roll around fast, using both hands to facilitate movement. Remember to use your feet to push/turn the body over. Think about how puppies and kittens play: you can learn a lot about judo grappling by watching their antics.

Practise all these movement exercises regularly – both for throwing and for grappling – and especially before you begin each training session. The length of time you spend on them depends on individual needs and preferences: some people need more time to experiment than others.

Basic principles

By now you should have discovered some basic principles as a result of your movement training. The following are the principles that I have found most useful: they should help to give a direction and purpose to your learning. Remember that they are by no means the only relevant principles: you may have discovered some important ones of your own.

• When you move *fast* it is difficult to generate much *force*. If you need force when moving fast, it can only be light and applied for a very short time (*see* fig. 4, page 7).
• A light force may be generated with one foot or two feet on the ground (*see* fig. 5, page 7). When you move slowly you may need to generate a lot of power: both feet must then be on the ground.
• If you can make your partner change direction sharply enough, or 'create' a moment in which he is standing still, that is a good time to attack.
• Your hands must be able to move independently of each other, like a pianist's, so that they can 'play' your partner in many different ways.
• The *space between the bodies* is an important factor. It is the 'no-man's-land' in which attacking and defensive moves take place. The player who controls that space is the winner.

If the movement is *fast*, then the space is usually *big* because the bodies tend to 'fly apart'. Any attacking action must be simple – there is no time for complicated moves, and the available power is limited because of the speed of movement (*see* type 1 techniques, pp 11–15).

If the movement is *slow*, the space between the bodies is *smaller* and therefore more manageable. Attacks should be strong and well organised (*see* type 2 techniques, pp 16–21).

Note that the space may be big because of body shape rather than speed of movement (*see* fig. 6, page 7). In this case, and if the speed is slow, the space should be kept the same (as if fixed) and the attack made slowly but with enough power to make the opponent roll into the ground (*see* type 3 techniques, pp 28–30).

Techniques – an introduction

Combination of the various elements of speed, power and space will determine what kind of technique you choose to use. Or, put another way, the technique you choose to try in a competitive situation will need to utilise the right mixture of these elements if it is to succeed.

In a 'live' situation, technique and movement are inseparable. However, if you are learning from a book, without the help of a coach, it is necessary to separate technique from movement in order to avoid confusion. In the following descriptions, therefore, I will describe the sequential actions as 'frozen moments', whereas you will be aware that they are actually parts of a moving reality.

As I do so, remember too that they are standard techniques for standard situations. There will be innumerable variations. It is important to realise that extreme situations (the fast and slow ends of the scale) offer the judo player few options – in terms of the technique that he chooses to use – while the standard or average situation offers many options. Understanding this, you will understand that your opponent will usually try to limit the number of options open to you by creating extreme situations.

If your partner has only one throw available to him, he will try to make you take up a certain position (usually by using various secondary attacks) to facilitate that throw. If he has several, he can try to move you around, increasing the likelihood that a suitable position for his attack will be reached.

Some general comments

• When you are learning the throwing action, your partner should stand straight, feet shoulder-width apart, right foot forwards or back according to the particular throw.

• In the case of grappling, your partner should lie on his right side.

• When a man is thrown towards his right side it is termed a right-handed technique. When he is thrown to his left it is termed a left-handed technique.

• I have divided the seven throws into three 'types', which in turn are based on the 'abstract' qualities of speed, power and space. When you are ready to start, you must decide first whether you prefer moving fast, at medium pace, or slowly. Depending on that decision, choose your technique.

If you are not sure what speed you prefer, go for medium. The group of medium-pace throws – type 2 – is the easiest group to perform because you have plenty of time and the movements are fairly easily controlled. There are of course many more than seven throws, and many of each type – but seven is enough to start with. You can learn the others later.

Techniques – type 1 (throwing)

- *Movement*: all around, fast; power, light; space between bodies, big (i.e. arms held loosely straight).
- *Stance*: the partner has his right foot forwards.

The foot trip (de-ashi-harai)

You are the attacker (on the right in fig. 7: on the left in fig. 8). Step well forwards with your right foot, past your partner's left foot. With your left foot, take his right foot through the space between your right and his left foot. To help the action, pull his right elbow in and down towards your moving right foot as you step forwards. This is a right-handed foot trip.

Free play

Move quickly around the mat, loosely but carefully. As your partner moves forwards, try to anticipate his action slightly and step your right foot into position as he begins to move his right foot forwards.

Note how, by stepping close to him, you compress the space between the bodies. This gives power to the sweeping action of the left foot. Because you should be moving fast, however, there is no time to get much power into the left foot or hand. Look at figs 7 and 8, and notice the relationship of the bodies throughout.

Figs 7–8   Imagine the partner moving forwards. Notice: the closeness of the two bodies as the foot sweeps; if the action foot (the left foot) takes the right foot sideways and backwards it will 'pull' the partner's left foot with it, so taking both feet off the ground. The attacker is looking where he is putting the man (always true). Remember fig. 4.

▲ *Fig. 7*   ▼ *Fig. 8*

11

The foot block (*sasai-tsurikomi-ashi*)

The starting position is as for the foot trip (*see* page 11). Step forwards with your left foot, past your partner's right foot (*see* fig. 9). Your right foot reaches out and blocks his left from moving forwards (*see* fig. 10). Notice how the attacker's hips move forwards and touch the opponent's right hip.

As the bodies touch, your right hand palls the opponent's head down, round and behind you (*see* fig. 11).

Note that in the foot trip your left hand is pulled down and across, with the right hand doing nothing. In the foot block it is the right hand that pulls down and round and the left hand that does nothing. Notice what the hands are doing – the right hand pulls the head down in the foot block, whereas the left hand pulls the *arm* down in the foot trip.

Remember how you pushed and pulled with your hands during your movement exercise training: use that training now.

◄ Fig. 9 The foot block. In this throw the partner can be moving forwards or backwards. For any attacking action the partner's head must be tightly controlled. Notice here how the partner's head is pulled down and round. The attacker's body is powerfully twisted; it rotates the partner over the trapped left foot.

▲ Fig. 10 Notice how the attacker's right foot is 'wrapped around' the left foot. The attacker's twisting body-weight drives the partner over the outside edge of the left foot.

▲ Fig. 11 The close-up shows the right hand pulling down and round, the left hand pushing through the partner's body, following the right hand.

Free play

As you are moving around, wait until your partner's left foot is moving backwards; step in with your left foot and finish it!

A note on falling

I had better break in here and talk about how you and your partner should fall down. It takes almost as much skill to fall down without hurting yourself as it does to throw! So you must practise falling down as well as your throwing and grappling techniques.

There are several different ways of falling safely; I will describe the most commonly used methods. You can learn other ways from experienced players, from your coach, or from your own (careful!) experimentation.

Round-the-side fall

This is the easy way of falling down (*see* pp 22–4 for other ways). The round-the-side fall is for when you are 'spilled' around the side of your attacker, hardly leaving the ground at all. The force of falling is spread over the whole length of the rolling body.

Stand as in fig. 12(a). Step forwards with your right foot, pivot on it, sit down and roll over (*see* figs 12(b–f)). After a few tries you will find this very easy. Try stepping forwards with your left foot, pivoting on it (i.e. turning the other way), sitting and rolling over. Try it with the legs-astride throw (*see* fig. 13). As your partner sweeps your right foot, simply sit down and roll over.

▲ *Fig. 12(a) Round-the-side fall.*

▲ *Fig. 12(b) shows the man pivoting to his right.*

▲ *Fig. 12(e)*

▲ *Figs 12(c) and (d)   should be done smoothly with no bumps or jerks.*

▲ *Fig. 12(f)   shows how the force of the 'fall' is absorbed by the rolling body.*

15

Techniques – type 2 (throwing)

- *Movement*: all around, at medium pace, with medium force, and with medium space between the partners.

The legs-astride throw (*tai-otoshi*)

Your partner (on the left in fig. 13) has his right foot back. Step forwards with your right foot (about half a stride); bring your left foot to it. Then step with your right foot forwards, blocking his right foot from moving. Pull with your left hand and push with your right, at the same time as your feet move.

Note how your body ends up approximately at right-angles to your partner's body (*see* figs 13(b) and 13(c)). As you pull and push with your hands, bend forwards from the waist. That should push him into the ground (*see* fig. 13(d)). You have thrown him!

Note too that the wide foot base makes this a very stable throw. For this reason it is one of the most popular.

Free play

Move around at a medium pace. As your partner moves backwards, follow his backward-moving right foot and step in to throw. He steps over the leg, sits and rolls down as in fig. 12.

▲ *Fig. 13(a) Legs-astride throw. Imagine the partner moving backwards, so the right foot is going back.*

▲ *Fig. 13(b) shows the attacker stepping across, after turning through 90 degrees, so that he throws the partner directly sideways.*

▲ *Fig. 13(c)*

▲ *Fig. 13(d) shows the partner stepping round, as in fig. 13 Have another look at fig. 5!*

The outside hook
(o-soto-gari)

Your partner (on the left in fig. 14) stands with his right foot forwards. Take a half-step forwards with your right foot (as you did in the legs-astride throw); bring your left foot back round behind your right foot, then hook your right leg in behind your partner's right leg (see fig. 14 (b)). As your feet move, pull with your left hand, push with your right hand and lean forwards. Down he goes!

Note that as you hook your right leg in, lean forwards and push and pull with the hands, he can swing his left foot back, sit and roll backwards.

Free play

Try the throw with your partner coming towards you (as he moves his right foot forwards). At this early stage of learning it is usually easier to use the round-the-side fall (see figs 14 (c) and (d), and fig. 12, pp 14–15); later on, however, you may have to use the over-the-top type (see fig. 18, p. 24).

▲ *Fig. 14(a)   The partner is moving forwards. This shows how far back the attacker keeps his left foot – this throws his weight forwards on to the partner, pushing him sideways and backwards. Before he does fall he pulls the right leg out and steps round as in fig. 12. Note the similarity with fig. 13. The main difference is in the use of the attacker's right leg.*

▲ Fig. 14(b)

▲ Fig. 14(c)

▲ Fig. 14(d)

The inside hook
(o-uchi-gari)

Your partner (on the left in fig. 15) stands with his left foot forwards. Starting as with the outside hook, move your right foot half-a-step forwards, bring your left foot back behind your right foot, and hook your right leg in behind your partner's left leg. As your feet are moving, pull with your left hand, push with your right hand. Bend forwards at the hips. Your partner then quickly lifts his left foot back, sits and rolls down (*see* figs 15(b), 15(c) and 15(d)).

Note that as you push him back it is more or less in the same direction as the previous throw – to his right side, back corner.

Free play

Try moving around freely, keeping your pace at fast/medium. Remember your movement training. How did you use your hands (together and separately)? How did you make your partner change direction? How did you make him stop? Add in these elements and then attempt a throw. Take it in turns.

20

▲ *Fig. 15(a)   Inside-leg-hook. Again the partner is moving forwards.*

▲ *Fig. 15(b)* shows the attacker pivoting on his right foot, bringing the left foot close behind it.

▲ *Fig. 15(c)* shows the right leg hooked inside the partner's left leg.

▲ *Fig. 15(d)* shows the partner being thrown over the outside edge of the right foot.

21

Another way of falling – 'over the top'

On pp 13–15 I explained how to fall down when you are 'spilled' around the side of the attacker, hardly leaving the ground at all. However, there will be times when your opponent tosses you up in the air and you have to land as best you can.

First type

Ask your partner to kneel down on hands and knees (*see* fig. 16(a)). He should keep the knees and hands apart for the greatest possible stability. Move up to him; hold his jacket. Put your chest to his back, push your head under his body and slowly roll over, controlling your speed with your hands (*see* fig. 16(b)). It should be easy. Try it several times. Make the feet hit the ground first (before the back). The idea is for the feet to absorb the force of the fall. For similar safety reasons, try not to let the head touch the floor at any time (*see* fig. 17).

Second type

If you are falling too fast to get your feet down first, your arms have to take the weight of the fall. To practise this, get your partner into the same position as before. Reach with your right hand and hold the back of his collar, then slide diagonally across his back. As you fall over, just before you hit the ground, strike the ground with your left arm (*see* figs 18(a–c)). Control the rate of fall with your right hand/arm. The arm serves the same purpose as the feet above.

As you become more confident, speed up. Grab the collar, dive over the kneeling body. Remember the purpose of your left arm – to take up the force of the fall. It must hit the mat just before your body. Now change sides. Then try it with a throw.

▲ *Fig. 16(a)*

Fig. 16(a–b) When starting, keep the roll-overs slow by using the hands and arms. Only speed up gradually. The main point: keep the head from touching the ground. When the roll-over is fast use the feet to break the fall by making them hit first, as in fig. 17.

▲ Fig. 16(b)

▲ Fig. 17

23

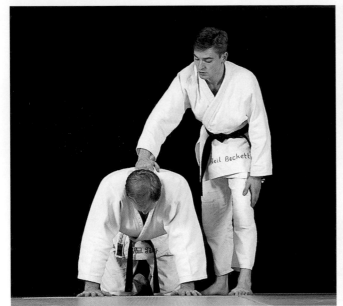

▲ Fig. 18(a)

▲ Fig. 18(b)

▲ Fig. 18(c)

Fig. 18 Over-the-top falling. The 'faller' slides over the back and drops to the floor, the right arm controlling the speed of the fall.

Fig. 18(c) shows the left arm absorbing much of the force. Do it both sides.

24

The shoulder roll (*ippon-seoi-nage*)

Your partner (on the left in fig. 19) stands up straight with his right foot back. You step well forwards with your right foot level with his left foot (*see* fig. 19(a)). Next swing your left foot round and back in the space between his feet. During this movement let go with your right hand. Into the space between the two bodies stick your bottom (*see* figs 19(b–d)). Your partner rolls over your back, as in the falling-down exercises (*see* fig. 19(e)).

You may wonder why you have to let go with your right hand. If you don't, the whole right arm will block your hips from moving into the correct position. It is important that you pull in very tight with the left hand as you release the right, to compensate for any loss of control. Look at fig. 19(f). Notice how the thrower's left hand has pulled the opponent in tightly, and how his kneeling position allows him more easily to roll his opponent over his back.

Free play

Move around easily. Remember that this is a medium-speed throw. Look out for when your partner moves backwards, taking his right foot back. As he does so, step forwards, pivot on your right foot, swing your hips through in front of his hips and drop on to your right knee. Roll him over, towards his right side. *Roll* him – that is very important. He can try the arm or the feet 'break-fall' – or both!

▲ *Fig. 19(a)   The shoulder roll: imagine the partner is moving backwards.*

▲ Fig. 19(b) shows the important point that after the turn the attacker's left foot must be behind the right foot.

Notice in figs 19(c) and 19(d) how the attacker lowers himself on to the right knee. The back left foot should be available to 'punch' the partner into the 'roll fall' as shown in fig. 19(e).

▲ Fig. 19(c)

▲ *Fig. 19(d)*

▼ *Fig. 19(e)*

▲ *Fig. 19(f)* *shows the actions of the hands.*

27

Techniques – type 3 (throwing)

- *Movement*: slow, with a lot of power.
- *Space*: big, made bigger by both of you half crouching.

The foot roll
(*tomoe-nage*)

Your partner (on the left in fig. 20) has his right foot slightly forwards. With your left foot, step forwards and outside his right (*see* fig. 20(b)). Using your left foot as a pivot, swing your body under him. Try to lie on his left foot (you won't be able to, but try!), on your left side. As you do so, place your right foot in his left groin. Pull down with both hands and, with the aid of your right foot, roll him over (*see* figs 20(b–e)).

In the early days of learning this throw your partner should not try to avoid it. As your (the attacker's) right foot comes up, he (the defender) should do a forward roll over the attacker's body, keeping his head well tucked in (so it does not hit the ground) and taking the fall confidently.

Free play

Move around slowly, in something of a crouch (*see* fig. 20(a)). As your opponent moves forwards (as his right foot moves forwards) step in and slide underneath him. Use your right foot to roll him over and forwards.

▶ *Fig. 20(a)   The foot roll: the partner can be moving forwards and backwards.*

▲ *In fig. 20(b) the wide-stepping left foot helps the body to swing into the position shown in fig. 20(c)* ▶

▲ Fig. 20(d) shows precisely where the attacker's right foot is placed.

▲ Fig. 20(e) shows how the partner falls, twisting sideways into the mat. Notice particularly that the attacker's back is not flat on the mat, but is lifting up. Look again at fig. 6.

Techniques – type 1 (grappling)

- *Speed* (rolling around): fast.
- *Power*: light.
- *Space*: big (because the movements are fast).

The straight-arm lock (*juji-gatame*)

Your partner is lying on his right side (*see* fig. 21(a)). Attack from his front. Kneel on your left leg, with your right foot on the ground. Catch his left wrist with your right hand. Half-stand on your right foot, swing your body round his arm into a straddle position (*see* fig. 21(b)), catching hold of his left wrist with your left hand (now both hands are holding his wrist firmly).

Lie back slowly and carefully (*see* figs 21(c–d)). As your back touches the ground, pull the straight arm over your left thigh. This is the arm lock (*see* fig. 21(d)). If you kept up the pressure you would break his arm! It is very, very important that you take great care when dropping back into the lock position.

As you swing round his left arm, sit on his left shoulder. This will keep you close to him, thus making the leverage stronger. Your partner should keep his left arm slightly – but very strongly – bent (so that it does not get straightened and damaged by accident). You can 'bend' it over your left or right thigh (not really bending it, because you would be in danger of breaking it!). A good tip is to keep his thumb pointing to the roof.

Convention

When your partner feels the pain of the lock begin – before then, if he can – he should tap/bang twice on the mat with his free hand. If he wants to, he can shout as well (but not too loudly). You must release him from the lock *immediately* at this point.

Free play

When you are comfortable with the movement, speed up the whole process. Step, catch the wrist, swing round and down. Be increasingly careful the faster you go, and listen out for his tap/shout of defeat. You must let go immediately.

Finally, try the whole lock 'in reverse' – i.e. the partner lies on his *left* side, and you start by holding his right wrist and stepping in with the left foot. Half-stand, swing the right leg round the arm, roll back and apply the lock. Hear/feel the tap/shout and stop (*see* fig. 23(c)).

◀ *Fig. 21(a)*

Fig. 21(b) ▶

◀ *Fig. 21(c)*

Fig. 21(d) ▶

Fig. 21   Straight-arm lock. Figs 21(a) and 21(b) show the attacker straddling the partner. Fig. 21(c) is the cautious roll back. Fig. 21(d)   shows the attacker lifting his hips to apply the lock. It is done in the red band of speed.

The bent-arm lock (*ude-garami*)

Your partner lies on his right side. Approach him from the side (*see* fig. 22(a)). Hold his left wrist with your left hand; now lay your right forearm on top of his left forearm and reach under his wrist to catch hold of *your own* left wrist (*see* fig. 22(b)).

Push him over on to his back, then press down with your left hand and lift his elbow up with your right elbow (*see* fig. 22(b)). You may well have to do some adjusting to get it just right. Change around. Try it with him on his left side and do the move in reverse.

Note that in grappling it is important that you are able to perform the hold with equal facility on either side of your partner's body.

When you roll him on to his back, use your body-weight and your feet to generate the necessary power. Notice the big space between the bodies at the start of the movement, and how little there is at the end – just as in throwing.

As with the straight-arm lock, let go of your partner's wrist immediately you hear/feel his tap or shout of defeat.

Free play

With your partner lying on his left side, and you facing his back, he rolls towards you. As he does, try the take/catch of the wrist – and off you go. Finally, mix up the straight- and bent-arm locks.

▲　*Fig. 22(a)*　　　▼　*Fig. 22(b)*

Fig. 22 Bent-arm lock. Fig. 22(a) shows the attacker's weight being used to push the partner flat on to his back. The hands are positioned correctly as that happens. Fig. 22(b) shows the location of the hands. To make the lock the partner's left wrist is pushed down, and the elbow raised.

Techniques – type 2 (grappling)

- *Speed*: medium.
- *Power*: medium.
- *Space*: medium (at the start of the action).

Note   This section contains strangles and chokes. The difference between the two is as follows. The *strangle* exerts pressure on the side of the neck, to stop blood from flowing to the brain. If this is maintained for about 30 seconds (or even less) the 'victim' will become unconscious. The *choke* exerts pressure on the windpipe, stopping the air from getting into the lungs. It will take a little longer for the victim of a choke to pass out. It will be obvious that great care must be taken when applying these techniques. Your partner must use his 'tap of surrender' very early on and you must release him *at once*.

The strangle from the opponent's front (*kata-juji-jime*)

Your partner is lying on his right side. You approach him from the front (*see* fig. 23(a)). Thrust your right hand inside his collar on his right side, with your fingers on the inside. Your left hand catches hold of his left collar, with your thumb on the inside. Try to touch your hands together at the back of his collar (*see* fig. 23(b)).

Now drop down, lying alongside him. 'Lift-pull' him on top of you (without releasing your grip). Pull down with both hands and raise your elbows. It is a scissor action, with his neck in the scissors. The edges of your wrists ought to be cutting into the side of the neck. When he feels it working he must tap immediately (he may not be able to shout this time). *See* fig. 23(c).

Note that the hands should touch at the back of the collar. This is to make the scissor effect as tight as possible. Push the wrists into the side of the partner's neck. It is very important that the partner tap defeat before any actual effect is felt on the neck.

Free play

Again, start from the other side of your partner. To reiterate, it is very important that you are able to perform the hold on both sides equally confidently. As you pull your partner on top of you, wrap your legs round him to make sure that he cannot get away (*see* fig. 24(b), page 36)!

▲ *Fig. 23(a)   Front strangle.*

Fig. 23(b)   shows the attacker at his most vulnerable – both his hands are close together making him very unstable. The attacker rolls to fig. 23(c) to regain the stability to strangle. See how important it is to know how to roll around; remember fig. 3? Notice how the right hand is tapping defeat in fig. 23(c).

▲ *Fig. 23(b)*

▶ *Fig. 23(c)*

The choke from the partner's rear
(okuri-eri-jime)

To make learning this technique a little easier, we will put your partner in a very artificial position. Once you have tried it out, you can experiment to find some of the many 'live' situations in which it can be applied.

Your partner sits as shown in fig. 24(a). You sneak up behind him. Put your right hand over his right shoulder and then deep into his left collar. Your left hand goes under his left arm and holds his right collar, about level with the armpit. You then 'push down' with your left hand and 'unwind' your right hand, cutting your right wrist hard into the front of your partner's throat. He will then need to tap.

Next, fall back, pull your partner on top of you, put your legs around him and hold him tight as shown in fig. 24(b).

Note the work done by the hands: one pulls down; the other pulls round. When you have your legs around him,

arch your back; this will in turn cause his back to arch and make the job of choking him easier (*see* fig. 25(b), page 38).

Free play

Try one of the throws. Pretend that the attack has failed and the attacker falls on to his hands and knees. Then jump on to his back and try the choke. Do not forget to practise it the other way so that you can push either your left or right hand into that choking position.

▲ *Fig. 24(a)*

Fig. 24   Rear choke. The usual time to attack with this choke is when the partner is laying face downwards. Try and make up a situation where you can do it. Chokes and strangles are usually done at a medium speed. It gives you time to think.   ▼ *Fig. 24(b)*

Techniques – type 3 (grappling)

- *Speed*: slow.
- *Power*: heavy.
- *Space*: small.

The side-pin (*yoko-shiho-gatame*)

Your partner lies on his right side. Approach him from the front (*see* fig. 25(a)). Hold his collar with your left hand (to control him – stop him running away!). Slip your right hand under his left arm, and use that leverage to turn him on to his back, freeing your left hand as you do so.

As he rolls on to his back, let your body move easily into the position shown in fig. 25(b). Your left hand goes over his left shoulder and grips his belt, while your right hand holds him somewhere at the top of his trousers (*see* fig. 25(c)).

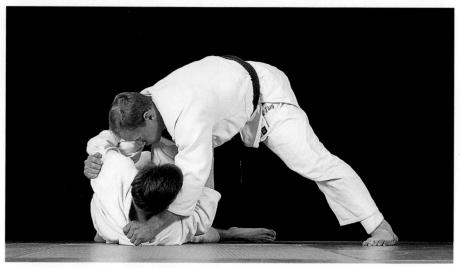

▲   *Fig. 25(a)*

Note   Try to focus your whole body-weight on to his right shoulder, pinning it to the ground. Your left hand pulls in tightly, restricting the movement of his head as much as possible. Your right hand is completely free, able to move anywhere to control the movement of his legs, hips and body. Notice how the movements change when you start with his right arm.

Fig. 25   Side-pin. As previously, the attacker's body-weight is used to flatten the partner on to his back. Fig. 25(b) shows the weight being focused on to the partner's right shoulder. Fig. 25(c) is the final tightening of the pin. The partner's head is tightly controlled (important in all attacks – throwing or grappling). The slow (blue) speed is being used here.

Free play

There are of course many types of pin in judo. It is the most popular way of winning when grappling. I picked this particular one because it is easy to get into the correct position. It also gives the greatest range of movement. As your partner struggles to escape, to dislodge you, you must be able to move around quickly to block each and every turn, however he may twist and wriggle. Do not try to remain still when you are pinning; be prepared to move before does in order to frustrate his efforts to break out.

▲ *Fig. 25(b)*

▲ *Fig. 25(c)*

The head-and-shoulder pin
(kesa-gatame)

Begin in the same way as in the side-pin, with your partner lying on his right side, your right hand under his left arm and your left holding on to his collar (*see* fig. 26(a)).

Turn him over on to his back, then sit in the space between the right side of his body and his right arm. Your left arm 'picks up' his right arm, and your right hand comes out from under his left arm and wraps around his head. Your two arms try to join together and in the process pin his shoulder to his head.

Note how the man on top – you! – has spread his legs widely (*see* fig. 26(b)). This is to give him a broad base and therefore a stable position when his opponent tries to break out. Notice too how the pinner's head is kept up. This helps him to see what is happening and move accordingly.

Note All the grappling attacks in the following photographs start from the same position, in order to make two points.

• If a throwing attack is not completed successfully and the partner just collapses into the ground (*see* fig. 5 on page 7), he frequently lands on his side. The thrower, with no hesitation, can attack with any grappling action instantly.
• With cunning, the attacker can disguise, right up to the last instant, which attack he intends to use. Indeed, he might not know himself – to the last instant!

Free play

Try to keep your arms and shoulders as strong as you can, but keep your legs as relaxed as possible so they can move easily to prevent any attempt to break out. Again, be prepared to attack from either side of your partner's body. You must be able to attack from any direction.

▲   *Fig. 26(a)*   ▼   *Fig. 26(b)*

Fig. 26 *Head-and-shoulder pin. A simple pin and, because the partner's head can be trapped (controlled) very effectively, a potentially very effective one.*

Tactics

When you begin to compete, either officially (under the rules of the organisation) or privately (under your own rules) you will need to have developed some *tactics*. Tactics may be defined as a series of attacks and defences that achieve a win (as defined by the rules).

The rules

The official rules, set by both national and international organisations, define how you may win a competition.

There are two kinds of score: *terminal* and *part-* or *non-terminal*. In throwing, a terminal score is achieved when the opponent lands fully on his back.

In grappling, if you can pin your opponent for 25 seconds, or with a strangle or a lock make him submit, both these afford a terminal score and signify the end of the match.

Part- or non-terminal scores can add up to a final decision, which is made by a referee, plus judges when necessary.

There are too many rules for me to list in this book. So let me sum up the true spirit of judo in three general rules:

● respect your opponent – have a responsible attitude to the conduct of the match
● do not take an unfair advantage of a momentary weakness of the opponent
● do not make derogatory or dramatic gestures to the opponent or spectators.

At a more mundane level, the rules dictate such things as the colour of the kit – usually white, but for international competition one player wears white and one blue for clarity

Remember: the performance should have integrity; behaviour should always be honourable.

Defence

For every attack there is of course at least one defence: indeed, there are far more defences than there are attacks. I have not included them in this book – it is more important at this stage to learn how to attack (which is very much harder than countering).

The main principle to bear in mind is that the best defence is either to attack first, or to avoid any attack before it even begins! This may seem impossible, but if you keep your wits about you and move easily and quickly around the mat you will find it surprisingly easy to sense when your opponent has decided to launch an attack. Then all you need to do is avoid being in the place he thinks you will be in when he does attack.

The success of any evasive action (either in throws or in grappling) before the attack, or of any defence after the attack has been launched, will depend on how quickly you can change the space between your two bodies as perceived by your opponent. If he wants and expects the space to be small, make it big. That will confuse him and muddle his techniques.

The best counter for a throw is often the throw itself. In the case of the foot trip, the attacked man can sweep his opponent's left foot away if he picks his own right foot up quickly enough. He can step over the blocking right foot and block the attacker's left foot. Likewise, when attacked with the outside-hook throw, he can drop the left foot back and throw the opponent instead.

Other throws need different counters. For example, if you are attacked with a foot-roll throw, knock your opponent's right foot aside and drop on him for a side-pin.

By now you should know how you prefer to move – fast, medium or slow – and therefore have a preferred technique. The ideal tactical situation for you is to have your opponent moving in your favourite pattern so that you can throw, pin, lock or strangle him with your favourite technique. Unfortunately, however, he will be doing everything to avoid getting into that situation! Your tactical job, therefore, is to force him or trick him into moving into that situation unintentionally.

Here you have to use your imagination. Be creative: attack with one technique, at its usual speed; your opponent – in order to prevent the attack – will change the speed and in doing so move at the speed that you need for your preferred technique. With practice you will quickly pick this up.

Champions can perform four, five, six attacks or more, each one involving varying degrees of speed, space and power, until the 'right' situation is finally reached. Of course, what happens often – as I'm sure you have realised – is that the change of speed and space is what your opponent also needs for his favourite attack. It is then a matter of who can think the fastest and move ahead of an ever-changing situation. This is what makes judo such an exciting and varied sport.

Players who prefer to grapple need to devise ways of getting their opponent from a standing/throwing position to a prone/grappling position. The choices are almost limitless. This is the main reason why it is better for you to learn in a moving situation – if you begin in a static position it is very difficult to add movement later (movement tends to distort technique). Adding technique to movement is preferable because you are much better able to modify technique having understood what movement is and how it affects thinking and performance.

The four established, traditional forms of training

Free play

You have been doing this already. It is a time of experiment, of trial and error, of finding out what you can do and how you can do it. It is competing under your own private rules, with no officials in charge.

Drills/structured training

Here, selected techniques are arranged in planned sequences in order to teach certain aspects of certain skills. Traditionally there are seven different sequences, designed by the founder of judo, Jigoro Kano (*see* pp 2, 47); but individuals can of course devise their own sequences for their own purposes.

The basic purpose of learning these structured sequences is twofold:

- to learn the biomechanics of technique
- to learn the morality of technique – that is, how to perform technical skills within the constraints of a competitive morality.

Competitive play

Players take part in competition that is controlled by widely accepted rules, implemented by at least one recognised official. Its purpose is to test the participants' ability to withstand the psychological stress of physical and moral constrictions.

Contest

Contest is formal competition, carried out according to nationally recognised rules and controlled by at least three officials and a supportive organisational group. It is what normally goes on at national and international tournaments.

The first purpose of contest is to test personal skills to the utmost, with the additional pressure of public attention, and to ascertain who can win according to the rules of that contest.

The second purpose – in terms of sequence only, and not of importance – is to test the honour of the individual: that is, to ascertain whether or not he can fight fairly and with impeccable sportsmanship.

Other forms of judo training

In the following forms of judo training, movement and technique remain the same. What differs is the purpose of performance.

Judo as a combat sport

This has been covered above.

Judo as a keep-fit activity

When joining movement and technique together during free play, the emphasis would be on cooperation (and not competition) so that the bodies are put through the widest possible range of actions to develop strength, speed and stamina.

Judo as a fighting system

Combat sports assume that the participants have an approximately equal degree of skill, and that superiority is judged by conventional criteria and on the skills that are produced within those criteria. Fighting judo assumes that the enemy does not know judo, and so the skills are applied to cause the maximum amount of injury. They are therefore taught and learned for that specific purpose.

It is for this reason – because judo can be used in this dangerous way – that the morality of the sport should be taught in training, no matter what type of judo the participant actually performs.

Judo as education

A strange purpose for a physical activity? Not really. There is much to be learned by the curious: the psychology of skill learning; teaching methodologies; the place of courage and discipline in personality development; the understanding of morality in a violent activity; the appreciation of a foreign culture. Judo is not the only sport that can teach you these things, but it does have its own special attractions.

The role of the judo teacher/coach

- To strive continually to improve his understanding of the skills of the game. This pertains especially to the analysis of skills and the comprehension of what comprises teaching and learning.
- To try to understand each individual in the training group so that the student is able to achieve his potential in the sport without losing sight of the greater things to be found outside it.
- To teach the morality of training and competition. Simply stated, this is a code of behaviour for the individual which both benefits and protects the group (of which the individual is a part) and the individual himself.

Glossary

Ideas and concepts

Aesthetics

Aesthetics is the study of beauty, and hence of ugliness. Beauty is an essential element in the development of physical skills; therefore it is beneficial to study beauty in all art forms as doing so will improve your performance. For example, the diagonal line emphasises the dynamic, or force, in an action image. How is this achieved? Look at the photograph on page 44. The imaginary line running through the two bodies is unstable and cannot be stationary, therefore it must be moving. When the line is vertical it is all stable, therefore there is no action. Look critically at other art forms.

Learning theory

Most authorities agree that, when acquiring a physical skill, learning should take place in circumstances as close to those in which the skill will eventually be used as is possible. In other words, you cannot learn to swim on dry land, only in the water. This is why I insist on an active moving situation when learning the throwing and grappling techniques.

When skills are analysed the components must be understood if learning is to take place. Do not simply accept the word of the coach (or of this book!). Question. Make them explain fully, so that you can understand.

Tradition

Tradition may be defined as a version of the truth that has evolved over a long period of time. It can help you, in the present, by offering a link with the past. It can also be a great nuisance because it gives you, in the present, an excuse for not thinking. Question tradition. Think for yourself.

Creativity/imagination

When performed by two individuals, any one skill will be different. Furthermore, the same skill performed by any one person will not be the same each time. You may need to learn standard forms of technique, as described in this book, but sooner rather than later you will need to develop your own skills. That requires imagination and creativity. In practice, this means that you should be able to imagine the standard forms extended into situations that you have not yet met, and be able to create skills for coping with those situations. Find out how artists create their art.

Morality

Morality may be defined as a code of behaviour that has evolved over time to benefit and protect the group which has generated that code. It has to do with duty, obligation, honour and justice, and therefore, indirectly, with freedom. The leader of the group – in judo, the coach – is the individual who explains the code of morality and the reason for it to others in the group.

Descriptions and definitions

Technique

Technique, in our context, may be defined as the biomechanical structure of the body, comprising a variable system of levers, powered by a variable range of power units (muscle groups) organised to produce a predetermined result.

Skill

Skill is the ability spontaneously to modify and adapt a technique in response to an unexpected, new situation. Skill is controlled by the psychic-psychological central power unit (the 'mind').

Break-outs

Break-outs are the methods used to escape from – *break out from* – the various grappling skills.

The best way to do this is to avoid the holds in the first place. Do not stay still for a moment when grappling, because stillness invites attack. For example, a pin can only score if you are pinned with your back to the ground. Practise never letting your back touch the ground; certainly never letting it rest on the ground. However, if you are caught (because of the other player's skill, and not because you have made a mistake!), the 'rule' is to make space between your body and your opponent's and then turn or twist into the space. By using that space you can 'break out'.

Strength/power

Power = muscular strength + body action.

You will often hear that judo does not require strength or power. This is nonsense, of course. Every physical action requires power; the great skill is to decide how much you need for any given situation. I have shown – and hopefully you have experienced this for yourself – that when you are moving fast, little power is needed. When you are moving slowly you need a great deal. A part of your skill involves learning how to generate a little or a lot of power – as and when you need it.

Other names in Japanese

- Throwing techniques: *nage-waza*
- Grappling techniques: *katame-waza*
- Free play: *randori*
- Drills/structured training: *kata*
- Competitive play: *shiai*
- Contest: *shobu*

Useful addresses

The British Judo Association
British Judo Association
Suite B
Loughborough Technology Park
Epinal Way
Loughborough
LE11 3GE
Tel: 0116 255 9669

The British Judo Council
1a Horn Lane
Acton
London W3 9NJ
Tel: 020 8992 9454

A final word

The inventor of judo was named Jigoro Kano (1860–1938). He was one of Japan's leading educationalists. He founded the Kodokan judo institute in 1882 and the Kobunkan cultural college. He was Principal of several very prestigious schools and colleges, Adviser to the Ministry of Education, and Japan's representative on the International Olympic Committee.

With the name of the founder of judo last in your mind, I wish you the greatest satisfaction and benefit from your voyage into an exciting and rewarding sport.

Index